THE SIX
BRANDENBURG CONCERTOS
and the
FOUR ORCHESTRAL SUITES

Johann Sebastian Bach

THE SIX
BRANDENBURG CONCERTOS
and the
FOUR ORCHESTRAL SUITES
in Full Score

From the Bach-Gesellschaft Edition

Dover Publications, Inc., New York

Published in Canada by General Publishing Company, Ltd.,
30 Lesmill Road, Don Mills, Toronto, Ontario.
Published in the United Kingdom by Constable and
Company, Ltd., 10 Orange Street, London WC 2.

This Dover edition, first published in 1976, is a republication
of music from two volumes of *Johann Sebastian Bach's Werke*,
originally published by the Bach-Gesellschaft in Leipzig. The
Brandenburg Concertos are from *Joh. Seb. Bach's Kammer-
musik. Dritter Band* (19th annual Bach-Gesellschaft volume,
for 1869, actually 1871; edited by Wilhelm Rust). The Orchestral Suites are from *Joh. Seb. Bach's Orchesterwerke* (31st
annual volume, for 1881, actually 1885; edited by Alfred
Dörffel).

The Summary of the Editors' Prefaces has been prepared
specially for the present edition.

International Standard Book Number: 0-486-23376-6
Library of Congress Catalog Card Number: 76-12016

Manufactured in the United States of America
Dover Publications, Inc.
180 Varick Street
New York, N.Y. 10014

Contents

BRANDENBURG CONCERTOS

ORCHESTRAL SUITES (OUVERTUREN)

page

Summary of the
Editors' Prefaces (1871 & 1885)

THE SIX BRANDENBURG CONCERTOS

Bach himself intended these concertos as a set. The basic source for the edition was the well-preserved autograph MS score, which once belonged to Johann Philipp Kirnberger, and later to his pupil Princess Amalie, sister of Frederick the Great; she bequeathed it to the Berlin *gymnasium* "Joachimsthal." The original parts of No. 5 are in the Berlin Royal Library.

The original title reads: "Six Concerts Avec plusieurs Instruments Dédiées A Son Altesse Royalle Monseigneur Crêtien Louis, Marggraf de Brandenbourg etc. etc. par Son tres-humble et tres obeissant serviteur Jean Sebastien Bach. Maitre de Chapelle de S. A. S. le prince regnant d'Anhalt-Coethen" (Six concertos with several instruments, dedicated to His Royal Highness Christian Ludwig, Margrave of Brandenburg, etc., by his very humble and obedient servant Johann Sebastian Bach, orchestral conductor of His Most Serene Highness the reigning Prince of Anhalt-Cöthen).

The original dedication reads: "A Son Altesse Royalle Monseigneur Crêtien Louis Marggraf de Brandenbourg &c. &c. &c. Monseigneur. Comme j'eus il y a une couple d'années, le bonheur de me faire entendre à Votre Altesse Royalle, en vertu de ses ordres, & que je remarquai alors, qu'Elle prennoit quelque plaisir aux petits talents que le Ciel m' a donnés pour la Musique, & qu' en prennant Conge de Votre Altesse Royalle, Elle voulut bien me faire l'honneur de me commander de Lui envoyer quelques pieces de ma Composition: j'ai donc selon ses tres gracieux ordres, pris la liberté de rendre mes tres-humbles devoirs à Votre Altesse Royalle, par les presents Concerts, que j'ai accommodés à plusieurs Instruments; La priant tres-humblement de ne vouloir pas juger leur imperfection, à la rigueur du gout fin et delicat, que tout le monde sçait qu'Elle a pour les piéces musicales; mais de tirer plutot en benigne Consideration, le profond respect, & la tres-humble obéissance que je tache à Lui temoigner par là. Pour le reste, Monseigneur, je supplie tres humblement Votre Altesse Royalle, d'avoir la bonté de continüer ses bonnes graces envers moi, et d'être persuadèe que je n'ai rien tant à coeur, que de pouvoir être employé en des occasions plus dignes d'Elle et de son service, moi qui suis avec un zele sans pareil / Monseigneur / De Votre Altesse Royalle / Le tres humble & tres obeissant serviteur / Jean Sebastien Bach. Coethen. d. 24 Mar. [Mai?] 1721" (To His Royal Highness Christian Ludwig, Margrave of Brandenburg, etc. Sire: Since I had the happiness, a few years ago, to play by command before Your Royal Highness, and observed at that time that you derived some pleasure from the small musical talent that Heaven has given me; and since, when I was taking leave of Your Royal Highness, you did me the honor to request that I send you some of my compositions: I have therefore, in compliance with your most gracious demand, taken the liberty of tendering my most humble respects to Your Royal Highness with the present concertos, arranged for several instruments, begging you most humbly not to judge their imperfection by the strict measure of the refined and delicate taste in musical pieces that everyone knows you possess, but rather to consider kindly the deep respect and the most humble obedience which I am thereby attempting to show to you. For the rest, Sire, I beseech Your Royal Highness most humbly to have the kindness to preserve your good will toward me and to be convinced that I have nothing so much at heart as to be able to be employed on occasions more worthy of you and your service, since I am with matchless zeal, Sire, Your Royal Highness' most humble and obedient servant, Johann Sebastian Bach. Cöthen, March [May?] 24, 1721).

Though the Brandenburg Concertos are a set by force of their 1721 date and dedication, they differ in genre and trend, and probably were composed at various times. Nos. 1 and 3 are more truly orchestral in style, and Bach later used their opening movements as symphonic introductions to cantatas (respectively, No. 52, "Falsche Welt, dir trau ich nicht," and No. 174, "Ich liebe den Höchsten von ganzem Gemüthe"). No. 5 is actually a clavier concerto, No. 4 a violin concerto. No. 2 has four solo instruments with equal roles, whereas No. 6 is in "quartet" style.

The first edition of these concertos was published by C. F. Peters of Leipzig in 1850.

CONCERTO NO. 1: The heading in the autograph MS reads: "Concerto 1ᵐᵒ à 2 Corni di Caccia, 3 Hautb: è Bassono, Violino Piccolo concertato, 2 Violini, una Viola è Violoncello, col Basso Continuo."

Page 8, m. 8: The second note in the Continuo is *a*-flat in the MS; altered here on the basis of the parallel passage (page 5, m. 3) and the cantata in which this movement was reused.

Page 13, m. 9: The MS has a natural sign before the fourth note of the Violino Piccolo; altered here on the basis of the Oboe part, page 12, m. 8.

CONCERTO NO. 2: The MS heading reads: "Concerto 2ᵈᵒ à 1 Tromba, 1 Fiauto, 1 Hautbois, 1 Violino concertati, è 2 Violini, 1 Viola è Violone in Ripieno col Violoncello è Basso per il Cembalo." The MS has a G-clef for the flute; this was characteristic of recorder notation.

Page 34, m. 2: In the MS, the solo Flute, Oboe and Violin have *d* as the fourteenth 16th-note, while the Violins of the *ripieno* have *f*. But on page 29, m. 3, they all have *f*.

Page 50, mm. 9 & 10: The MS gives *a*-flat in the solo voices, *a* in the *ripieno*.

CONCERTO NO. 3: The MS heading reads: "Concerto 3ᶻᵒ a tre Violini, tre Viole, è tre Violoncelli col Basso per il Cembalo."

Page 67, m. 4: In the MS the third note in Violin II is *e*, which creates an octave with Viola I.

Page 76, m. 1: In the MS the eighth 8th-beat in Violin II is *d*.

CONCERTO NO. 4: The MS heading reads: "Concerto 4ᵗᵒ à Violino Principale, due Fiauti d'Echo, due Violini, una Viola è Violone in Ripieno, Violoncello è Continuo."

This is certainly a violin concerto, as proven, for example, by the figures in the last measures on page 77, the double stopping on page 88 and the use of the open E and A strings on pages 108 & 109. Bach reworked this as an F Major clavier concerto.

Page 80, m. 10: In the MS Flute II had *a* as the fourth and fifth notes; this did not correspond to any of the parallel passages.

CONCERTO NO. 5: The MS heading reads: "Concerto 5ᵗᵒ â une Traversiere, une Violino principale, une Violino è una Viola in ripieno, Violoncello, Violone è Cembalo concertato." The editor of the 1850 Peters first edition preferred the MS parts to the MS score when readings diverged; usually parts are to be preferred, as coming later and embodying improvements, but in this case the autograph MS score is a very clean and neat later copy. The dynamic marks are fuller and more accurate in the score; another factor showing that the MS score we possess is later than the MS parts is a correction in it made by Bach: attempting to avoid parallel octaves with the solo Violin, he changed one bar of the Viola line (page 117, m. 11 of this volume) to read Since, however, this is even worse, creating fifths with the Clavier, the first form of the passage has been adopted here. Passages where the MS score has here been preferred to the MS parts are as follows:

Page 121, m. 4: page 126, mm. 2 & 5; and page 144, mm. 16–18: In the parts the Violone has full-measure rests.

Page 131, m. 6; page 132, m. 7; and page 133, mm. 1 & 5: In the parts the 32nd-note figure does not occur, and there are merely 16th-notes.

Page 134, mm. 6–12: In the parts the low *a* is marked to be held throughout.

Page 149, mm. 10–13 are missing in the parts, where after m. 9 the passage resumes:

CONCERTO NO. 6: The MS heading reads: "Concerto 6to à due Viole da Braccio, due Viole da Gamba, Violoncello, Violone e Cembalo."

Page 158, m. 3: In the MS, Viola I has *e* instead of *e*-flat, and Viola da Gamba I has

 for the second half of the measure.

THE FOUR ORCHESTRAL SUITES

Bach referred to this set as "Ouverturen," which strictly applies only to the first movements. "Suite" or "Partie" (partita), though perfectly appropriate for these pieces, was then usually applied to similar works for individual instruments. Each of the orchestral suites begins with a "French overture": a slow, serious section followed by a faster, fugal one, which leads back to the first section. Other movements are usually in dance forms: sarabandes, gavottes, courantes, etc. The order of the Suites in this edition [which established the traditional numbering] is chronological, as far as can be determined. Nos. 1 and 2 are from the Cöthen period; the others, more richly orchestrated, are probably from the years 1729 to 1736 in the Leipzig period.

SUITE NO. 1: The sources were a MS score, old MS parts (the most reliable source) and more recent MS parts (with the thorough-bass figures adopted in this edition) that were based on the MS score, all in the Royal Library, Berlin; and the first edition (C. F. Peters, Leipzig, 1853), based on the older MS parts.

Page 181, m. 1: The tempo indication ("Grave"), as well as the "Vivace" on page 182 (last measure of center system) seem to have been written into the MS later by another hand.

Page 181, m. 2: In the Violin II part, the second note is *c* in the MS score.

Page 182, m. 1: The figure [music] in the third quarter is to be understood as

[music] here and elsewhere.

Page 191, m. 3: Here and in the last measure of the movement, the MS parts lack the 8th-rest.

Page 198, m. 1: In the older MS parts, Oboe I has

SUITE NO. 2: The sources were Bach's original autograph MS parts, a score written by S. Hering, and more recent MS parts, all in the Royal Library, Berlin; and the first edition (C. F. Peters, Leipzig, 1853), based on the autograph parts.

Page 202, m. 1: No tempo indication at the beginning in the sources, but Bach himself wrote in the "Lentement" on page 209.

Page 202, m. 4: On the second quarter, the bass figuring reads "7" in the autograph parts, " $^6_4{}_3$ " in the Hering score, and " $^6_4{}_2$ " in the first edition.

Page 205, next-to-last measure: The autograph Violin I part has e-sharp on the third quarter, the other sources have d (like the flute).

SUITE NO. 3: The sources were old MS parts (the most important source; three parts are in Bach's hand), other MS parts and a more recent MS score, all in the Royal Library, Berlin; the first edition (C. F. Peters, Leipzig, 1854), based on the older MS parts; and the 1866 edition (Bartholf Senff, Leipzig), altered for modern instruments by Mendelssohn, who revived the work in 1838.

Page 218, m. 1: The tempo indications "Grave" (here) and "Vivace" (page 220, last measure in upper system) were added in the older MS parts by C. P. E. Bach. In the latter place, J. S. Bach wrote "viste" in the Violin I part.

Page 218, m. 5: On the second quarter, the older MS parts give both Oboes

, unlike Violin I.

Page 235: In the older MS parts, the meter indication of Gavotte II is "2."

Page 238, m. 6: On the first quarter, the older MS Violin II part has a, f-sharp; in the first edition, b, f-sharp.

SUITE NO. 4: The sources were a MS score copy by Fischhof (careless; mentions three Flutes instead of three Oboes) in the Royal Library, Berlin; a set of MS parts written by Penzel (careless) owned by the singer Hauser in Karlsruhe; the Peters edition of 1881, based on Fischhof and "the Gleichauf copy according to Schelble," owned by the Peters firm. This work was long considered as only doubtfully by Bach, until the 1876 discovery of Cantata No. 110, "Unser Mund sei voll Lachens," in which the first movement of the Suite was reused for the prelude and opening chorus, the chief alteration being the addition of the vocal parts.

Page 244, mm. 2 (last note) & 3 (first note): Trumpet II has c, g in Peters; f, f in the cantata.

Page 244, m. 3 (last quarter): In the MSS, the Oboes have an 8th-rest and an 8th-note; rhythm changed here (and page 245, m. 2, Violin II and Viola) on the basis of the cantata.

Page 244, m. 6 (fourth 8th-beat): In the MSS and Peters, Oboe II has c-sharp; changed to b here on the basis of the cantata.

Page 245, m. 2: For the first note in Violin II, Peters has d.

Page 245, m. 3: Several notes are different in the cantata; e.g., Oboe I and Violin I have b for the last note.

Page 245, m. 8: The Viola part is different in the cantata.

Page 246, m. 5: Several notes different in cantata.

Page 246, last measure: In Peters, on the fifth 8th-beat, Oboe II and Violin II have e.

Page 247, m. 6: The Viola's next-to-last note is *f*-sharp in Peters (like Oboe III).

Page 248, m. 6: For the first third of the measure, Peters gives Violin II ♪♪♪

Page 249, m. 2: In Peters and the cantata, Oboe I has *d*-natural as the sixth and eighth notes.

Page 250, m. 11: In Peters and the cantata, the Bassoon and Continuo have *g*-sharp as the fifth note.

Page 253, m. 2: In Peters, Oboe III has a full-measure rest.

Page 253, first third of m. 4: In Peters and the cantata, the Bassoon follows the Continuo: *b, d, f*-sharp.

Page 253, first third of m. 8: The MSS and Peters have for Oboe II ♪♪♪ This has been changed to *b, b* on the basis of Violin II, and this is also to be found in the cantata.

Page 254, mm. 4 & 5: The Oboe III part given here is as in the cantata; different in Peters.

Page 254, m. 7: In the cantata, on the fifth 8th-beat, Violin I has *f*-natural.

Page 254, first third of m. 10: The cantata gives the Bassoon and Continuo ♪♪♪

Page 255, mm. 3 ff.: In Peters and the Cantata, the Bassoon and Cello parts are interchanged.

Page 257, fifth 8th-note of m. 2: In Peters and the cantata, Violin I has high *e*.

Page 257, last third of m. 4: In Peters and the cantata, Oboe III has *f*-sharp, *b*.

Page 258, m. 8: In Peters the first Violin II note is *f*-sharp.

Page 259, m. 2: In the cantata the first Oboe III note is *a* and the first Violin II note is low *d*.

Page 259, m. 4: The last Oboe III note is *b* in Peters, and the last Viola note is *b* in Peters and the cantata.

Page 259, m. 5: In Peters the last Viola note is *e*.

Page 259, m. 9: In the cantata the second Viola note is *g*.

Page 260, m. 9: The third Viola note is *b* in Peters and the cantata.

Page 261, m. 7: In Peters the first Oboe III note is *c*-sharp.

Page 264, m. 8: In Peters both Oboe III notes are a third higher.

Page 267, m. 2: In Peters, Violin I follows Oboe I exactly.

Page 267, m. 6: In Peters the first Continuo note is *a*. From the Menuet to the end, Peters lacks the Bassoon part.

Page 270, fourth measure from the end: In Peters the last Oboe I and Violin I note is *g*.

Page 272, fourth 8th-beat of m. 2: In Peters, Oboe III has *f*-sharp.

Page 272, m. 9: On the third 8th-beat, Peters gives Oboe III *e*. On the fourth 8th-beat, Peters gives the Viola *d*.

Brandenburg Concerto No. 1 in F Major

Adagio.

Allegro.

Adagio.　　　　　(Allegro.)

Adagio.

Adagio.

Menuetto.

26

Fine.

Trio a 2 Oboi e Fagotto.

Oboe I.
Oboe II.
Fagotto.

Menuetto da Capo, e poi la Polacca.

Polacca. Tutti i Violini e Viola, ma piano. Violino piccolo si tace.

Violino I.
piano
Violino II.
piano
Viola.
piano
Continuo.
piano

Menuetto da Capo, e poi il Trio.

Trio a 2 Corni e 3 Oboi all'unisono.

Corno I.

Corno II.

Tutte le Oboi.

Menuetto da Capo sino alla Fine.

Brandenburg Concerto No. 2 in F Major

Tasto solo

accomp.
6

piano

piano

piano

piano

piano

piano

6
4
2

7

42

44

Brandenburg Concerto No. 3 in G Major

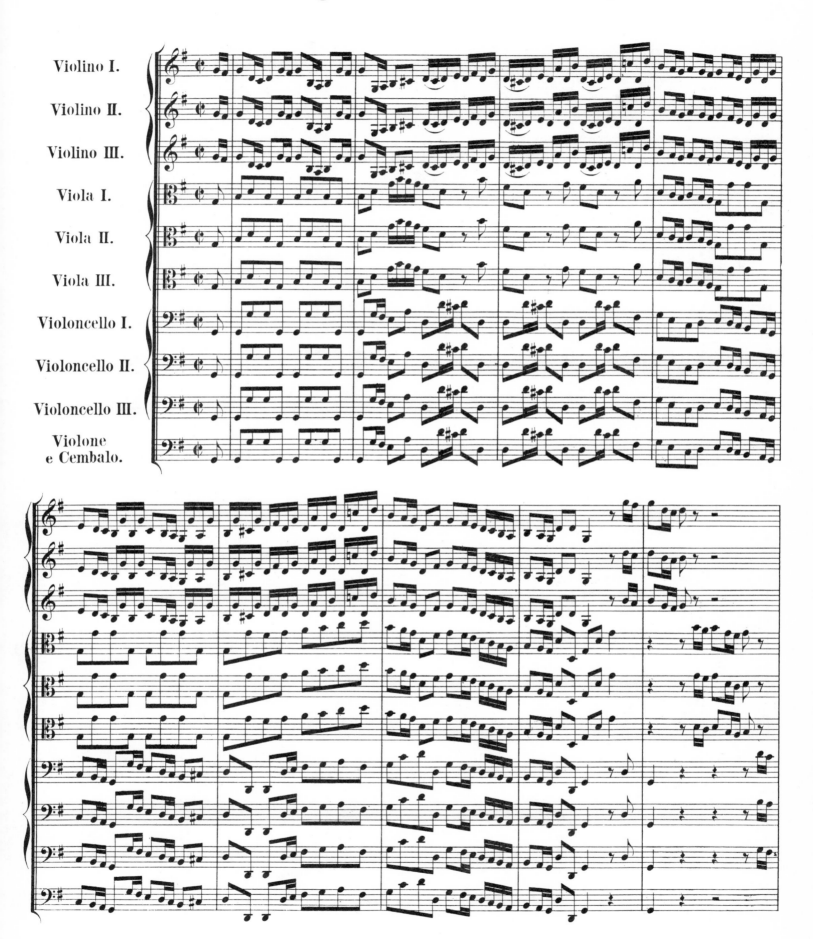

Adagio.

Allegro.

Brandenburg Concerto No. 4 in G Major

Andante.

Presto.

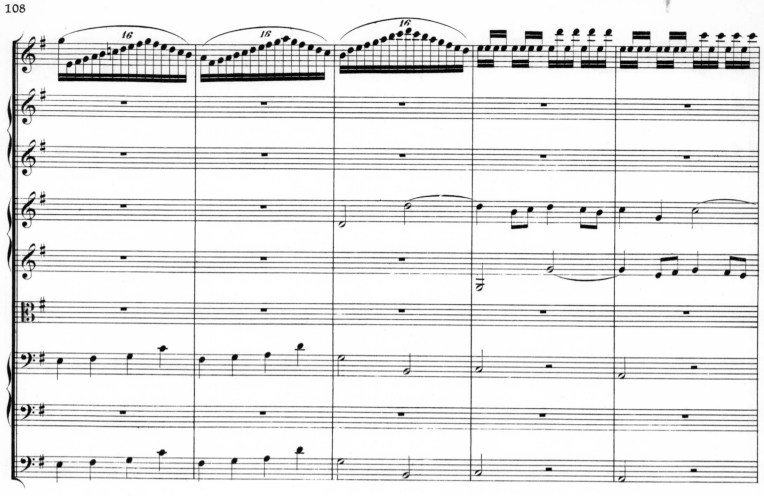

Brandenburg Concerto No. 5 in D Major

Cembalo solo senza stromenti.

138

Brandenburg Concerto No. 6 in B-flat Major

Adagio ma non tanto.

Allegro.

Orchestral Suite No. 1 in C Major

182

Courante.

Gavotte I. alternativement.

Gavotte II.

Forlane.

Gavotte I. da Capo.

196

Menuet I. alternativement.

Menuet II.

Bourrée I. alternativement.

Bourrée II.

Bourrée I.da Capo.

Passepied I.

Passepied II.

piano

Passepied I. da Capo.

Orchestral Suite No. 2 in B Minor

Rondeau.

Sarabande.

Bourrée I.

Bourrée II.

Bourrée I.
da Capo.

Polonaise.

Moderato e staccato.

lentement

piano   forte

Double.

piano

Polonaise
da Capo.

Menuet.

216

Badinerie.

Orchestral Suite No. 3 in D Major

220

Air.

Violino I.

Violino II.

Viola.

Continuo.

Gavotte I.

Tromba I.
Tromba II.
Tromba III.
Timpani.
Oboe I.
Oboe II.
Violino I.
Violino II.
Viola.
Continuo.

Gavotte II.

Gavotte I. da Capo.

Bourrée.

Gigue.

Orchestral Suite No. 4 in D Major

258

Bourrée I.

Bourrée II.

264

Bourrée I. da Capo.

Gavotte.

Menuet I.
alternativement.

Menuet II.

Trio a 2 Violini, Viola e Continuo.

270

Réjouissance.

Menuet I. da Capo.